Daily Positivity: Affirmations for Black Trans Folks

By

Mx. Renae M. Taylor

Dedication

Dedicated to The Taylor Family

For your unwavering love, resilience, and support. May these affirmations honor the strength and spirit that binds us, and may they serve as a testimony to the courage, pride, and beauty we carry forward together!

About the Author

Mx. Renae Taylor is an inspiring individual with a rich background in activism and advocacy. As a 49-year-old Black, Disabled, Non-Binary Trans Organizer based in Memphis, Tennessee, Renae has dedicated her life to promoting transgender rights, HIV prevention, and social justice.

Renae, who uses both they and she pronouns, hails from Tupelo, MS. Since 2000, she has been a relentless advocate for the transgender community, travelling worldwide to raise awareness about transgender rights, needs, and visibility. Renae is a consultant for the Transgender Community, working towards creating a more inclusive and equitable future for all Black and Brown people with multiple intersecting identities.

In addition to her advocacy work, Renae is an HIV Prevention Educator and Activist, actively associated with various HIV prevention organizations. Her commitment to this cause is further exemplified by her involvement with the regional planning group as part of the state of TN's HIV prevention program.

Renae's commitment to social justice, extensive experience, and involvement in various organizations position her as a powerful force in the ongoing fight for equity and justice. Her keynote speeches and participation in conferences showcase her leadership in pursuing a more inclusive and equitable future for all.

Prologue

In a world where identity and existence are often challenged, *Affirmations for Black Trans Folks* offers a voice of strength, resilience, and self-celebration for Black trans individuals. This collection of affirmations is crafted to uplift, inspire, and reaffirm the beauty and power inherent in every Black trans person. It acknowledges the struggles while empowering the reader to embrace their identity with pride, knowing they are worthy of love, respect, and peace. May these words serve as a daily reminder of the light within you, a beacon to guide you through each challenge, and a source of courage to live boldly and unapologetically.

Table of Contents

Daily

Affirmations

for

Black

Trans

People

I am powerful beyond measure, and my existence is a testament to resilience and courage.

I honor and celebrate my identity every day, knowing that I deserve love, respect, and joy.

I am the embodiment of beauty, strength, and grace, and I embrace every part of who I am.

My voice matters, and I speak my truth with confidence and clarity, knowing that I am making a difference.

I am rooted in the rich history of my ancestors, drawing strength from those who came before me and paving the way for those who will follow.

I deserve spaces that affirm and uplift me, and I have the right to walk away from anything that does not honor my worth.

Every day, I grow stronger in my identity, knowing that I am fearfully and wonderfully made.

I am worthy of all the good

things that life has to offer,

and I will not settle for

anything less than what I

deserve.

My existence is an act of

revolution, and I am proud of

the person I am becoming.

I love and accept myself fully,

knowing that I am perfect just

as I am.

I find peace in knowing that I am not alone and I am part of a community that supports and uplifts me.

I release any fear or doubt that
tries to hold me back,
embracing the limitless
possibilities that lie ahead.

I am in control of my destiny, and I create the life that I desire with intention and purpose.

I forgive myself for any past mistakes, understanding that they are part of my growth and evolution.

I am a beacon of light, and my presence brings love, joy, and positivity to the world around me.

Affirmations

for

Black

Trans

Folks

Rooted

in

Black

Liberation

I am a revolutionary spirit, carrying the torch of Black liberation and trans freedom within me. My existence is a testament to our collective fight for justice.

I stand on the shoulders of my ancestors, and I honor their legacy by living authentically and unapologetically in my truth.

My identity is a powerful act of resistance, and I embrace it fully, knowing that my liberation is intertwined with the liberation of all Black people.

I am part of a long tradition of Black resilience and strength, and I draw power from our shared history of overcoming oppression.

My life is an embodiment of freedom, and I will not allow anyone to diminish my light or silence my voice.

I am worthy of the same rights, dignity, and respect that my ancestors fought for, and I will continue their fight with pride and determination.

I celebrate my Blackness and

my trans identity as beautiful,

powerful, and revolutionary.

Together, they make me whole

and unstoppable.

I deserve to live in a world free from oppression, where my existence is not just tolerated but celebrated. I will work to create that world.

I claim my right to joy, love, and happiness, knowing that these are essential parts of my liberation and the liberation of my community.

My journey is a reflection of the ongoing struggle for Black trans liberation, and I am committed to advancing that struggle with courage and compassion.

I honor the intersection of my Blackness and trans identity, knowing that both are integral to who I am and to the broader fight for justice.

I am unbreakable, drawing strength from the revolutionary movements that came before me and those that continue to rise today.

I am part of a global community of Black trans folks, and together, we are creating a world where we can all thrive in freedom and peace.

I embrace my role in the movement for Black liberation, knowing that my voice and actions contribute to the collective power of our people.

I deserve to live fully, freely, and without fear. I claim my space in this world as a Black trans person with pride and conviction.

Affirmations for Black Trans Folks Based on Black Lives Matter Principles

I affirm that my Black trans life matters. I am deserving of love, safety, and respect in every space I enter.

I am a vital part of my community, and my voice, experiences, and identity are crucial to the fight for justice and equality.

I honor the interconnectedness of all Black lives, recognizing that my liberation is tied to the liberation of all Black people, especially the most marginalized among us.

I celebrate my identity and the beauty of my existence, knowing that I am worthy of joy, peace, and fulfillment.

I reject all forms of anti-Blackness and transphobia, and I stand firmly in the belief that my life is sacred and irreplaceable.

I claim my right to live without fear of violence or discrimination. I am committed to creating a world where Black trans lives are protected and cherished.

I am empowered by the
strength of my ancestors and
the collective power of the
Black Lives Matter movement.
Together, we are unstoppable.

I embody the principles of love, empathy, and humanity, and I extend these values to myself and my community in all that I do.

I honor the diversity within the Black community, embracing all expressions of Blackness and celebrating the richness of our collective identities.

I am a leader in the movement for Black liberation, and I use my voice and actions to uplift, protect, and empower Black trans lives.

I believe in the importance of restorative justice, and I advocate for healing and accountability in my relationships and community.

I deserve to live in a world that affirms my existence and honors my contributions. I will continue to fight for that world with courage and determination.

I find strength in the principle of collective care, knowing that I am part of a community that supports and uplifts one another.

I am a living testament to the resilience and power of Black trans people, and I will continue to thrive despite any challenges I face.

I affirm that my story, my journey, and my dreams are important. I will not be silenced, and I will continue to speak my truth boldly and unapologetically.

Made in United States
Cleveland, OH
10 April 2025

15982468R10057